FOR MY FAMILY.
THANKS FOR ALL YOUR
ENCOURAGEMENT.

A tiny, winged insect;
my swarm's called a ghost,
and anything rotten, is what I like most.

I am a...
GNAT

This clever social insect,
when joined by many friends,
can build a bridge by joining its
fronts on to its ends.
And when they all get hungry,
they form a single line,
and march into their tunnel for
evening suppertime.

I am a...
ANT!

It's bioluminescence that makes me
glow so bright,
that you can see me blinking on a
warm, dark summer night.
Some children try to catch me and
put me in a jar.
They think that I am special...a tiny,
sparkling star.

I am a...
FIREFLY!

I get a bad rap from all it would seem.
They say that I bite, and that I am mean.
But I am important, and not to be dread.
I clean up an animal after it's dead.

I am a...
FLY!

You have the hardiest appetite.
You eat all the crops and plants in sight.
You hop away at the end of day,
rub your hindlegs together, and music you play.

You are a...
GRASSHOPPER!

This insect is no lady — it could
be a boy or girl.
You can't tell by the polka dots;
there isn't any curl.
Lovely you may call it, but to me
the prettiest sight,
is when I see it feasting on an
aphid or a mite.

I am a...
LADYBUG!

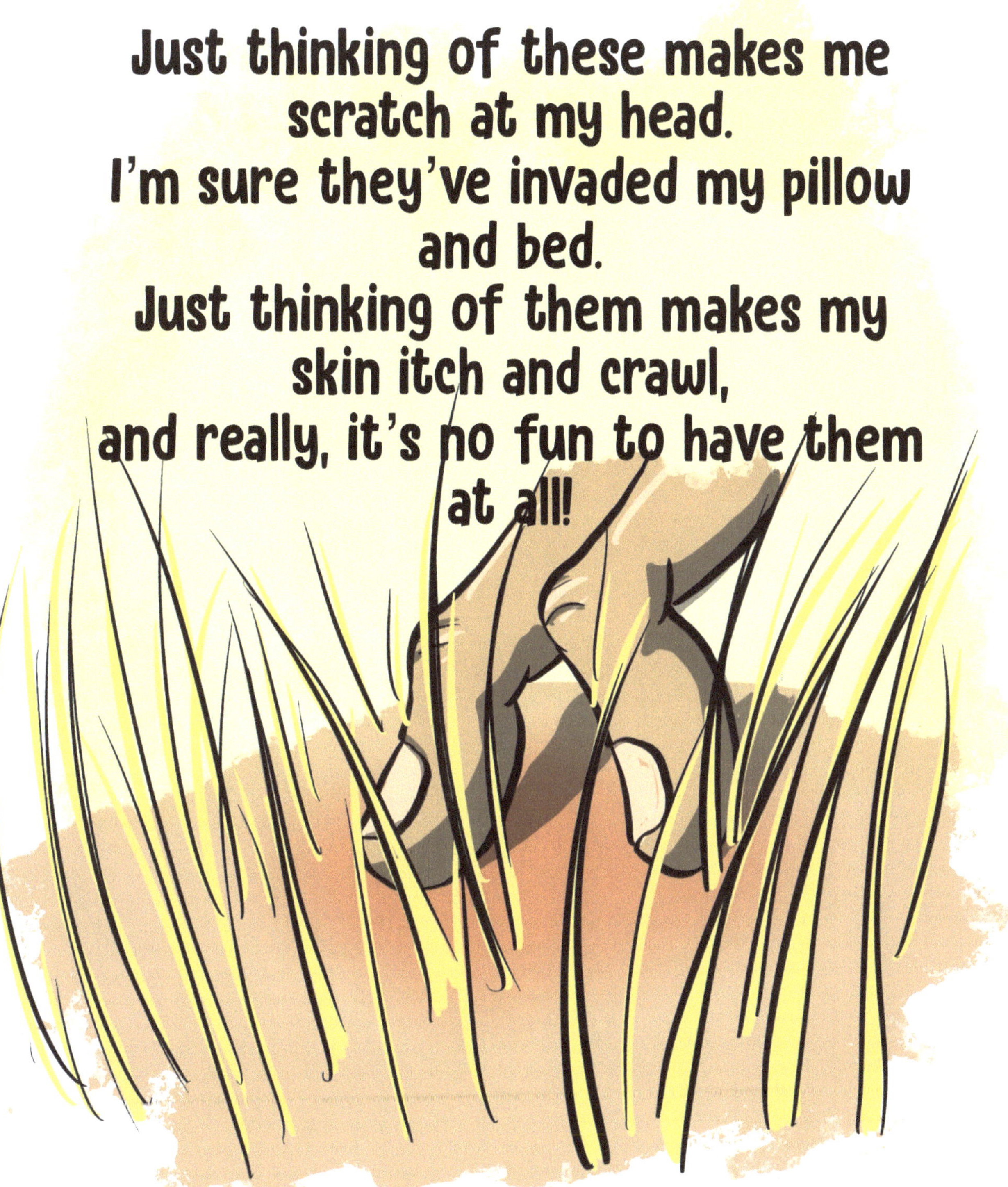

Just thinking of these makes me
scratch at my head.
I'm sure they've invaded my pillow
and bed.
Just thinking of them makes my
skin itch and crawl,
and really, it's no fun to have them
at all!

You are...
LICE!

My arms are folded like in prayer.
To others it would seem I care.
But then I strike with lightning speed,
and grab the prey on which I feed.

I am a...
PRAYING MANTIS!

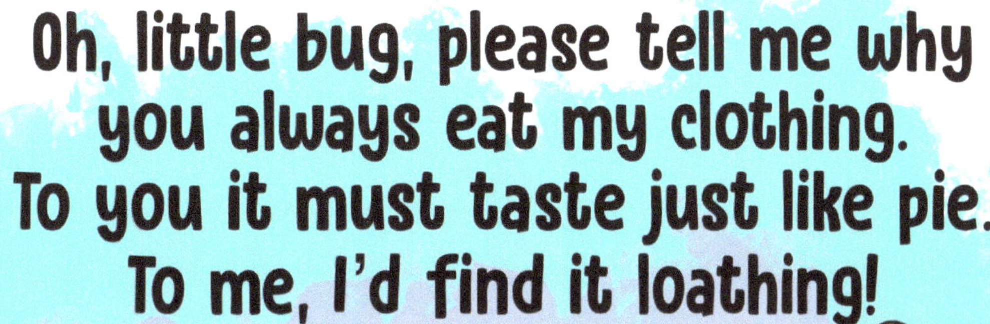
Oh, little bug, please tell me why
you always eat my clothing.
To you it must taste just like pie.
To me, I'd find it loathing!

You are a...
MOTH!

Because of my name, you'd think I could swim,
instead, I have legs; a body that's slim.
I scurry across the floor mighty fast,
and if we should race…you would come in last.

I am a...
SILVERFISH!

I bounce, and spring, and jump in the air,
I land, and make a home in the hair,
of Fetch the dog or Fluffy the cat,
then bite, and feed, and grow very fat.

I am a...
TICK!

When I'm standing still, I look like a stick,
but then I start walking—is it a trick?
My camouflage is impressive to most,
but I am quite shy, and don't want to boast.

I am a...
WALKING STICK!

I build mud nests,
and paper ones too.
I hang them up high,
then swoop and sting you!

I am a...
WASP!

I zip all around and plan my attack—
a nice juicy arm, a wide, open back.
I buzz in your ear; I roll, and I pitch.
I bite, then leave you to scratch at your itch.

I am a...
Mosquito

ABOUT THE AUTHOR
NANCY DORT ROSSOW, PH.D

IS A RETIRED SCHOOL
PSYCHOLOGIST AND UNIVERSITY INSTRUCTOR. SHE WAS A FORMER
BIOLOGY TEACHER, AND CURRENTLY WRITES NOVELS AND PICTURE
BOOKS. SHE IS THE MOTHER OF TWO GROWN WOMEN AND SPLITS HER
TIME BETWEEN FLORIDA AND COLORADO. HER DEBUT NOVEL,
A DEEP PLACE OF GRACE, IS AVAILABLE IN

YOUNG BOOKWORMS GIFT AND BOOKSTORE, AND
ONLINE AT AMAZON.COM, AND YOUNGBOOKWORMS.COM.

ABOUT THE ARTIST

I LOVE TO CREATE, WHETHER IT IS OUT OF MY OWN
IMAGINATION OR THE IMAGINATION OF OTHERS. NOTHING
BRINGS ME MORE JOY THAN TO SIT IN FRONT OF AN
EMPTY PAGE AND START TO MAKE IDEAS A REALITY!

I HAVE BEEN ILLUSTRATING SINCE I CAN REMEMBER. WHETHER IT'S
CHILDRENS BOOKS, GRAPHIC NOVELS, BOARD GAMES, OR MOVIE SETS, I
LOVE EVERY ASPECT OF CREATING SOMETHING NEW.

WWW.JUSTINDUNNILLUSTRATIONS.SQUARESPACE.COM